HISTORY · IN · STONE

ANCIENT EGYPT

ANDREW LANGLEY

Silver Dolphin

San Diego, California

Author: Philip Steele
Editors: Jayne Miller and Clare Oliver
Designer: John Jamieson
Art editor: Martin Aggett
Art director: Terry Woodley
Picture research: Image Select International
Illustration: Kevin Maddison, Julian Baker, and
Danny McBride

Silver Dolphin Books

An imprint of the Advantage Publishers Group
5880 Oberlin Drive
San Diego, CA 92121–4794
www.advantagebooksonline.com

Copyright © Quarto Children's Books, 2001

ISBN 1-57145-552-3

Printed in China

1 2 3 4 5 06 05 04 03 02

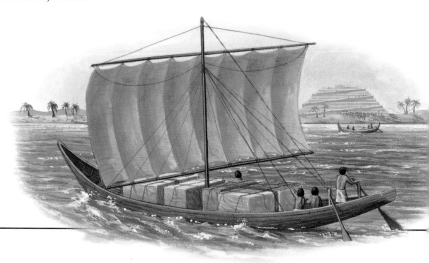

CONTENTS

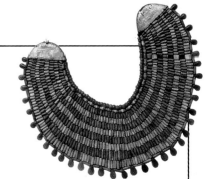

WHO WERE THE ANCIENT EGYPTIANS?

About 5,000 years ago, a great empire grew up on the banks of the Nile River in Egypt. This empire survived for nearly 3,000 years—longer than almost any other civilization. During that time, the ancient Egyptians built some of the most gigantic and amazing structures the world has ever seen, including the incredible Egyptian pyramids. The Egyptians also developed a complex religion, created their own calendar and a special type of picture-writing, and amassed fabulous wealth in gold and precious stones.

THE RICHES OF THE RIVER
The Nile River gave life to what was otherwise a dry and barren area. It entered Egypt from the south, roaring over rocky rapids known as the First and Second Cataracts. The Nile flowed north for more than 620 miles (1,000 km) through a long, narrow valley, eventually reaching the Mediterranean, where it fanned out into a huge delta.

EARLY SETTLERS

The first settlers arrived in the area now called Egypt about 7,000 years ago. The country around the river was lush, with plenty of rain. Grass and low trees grew, and rivers flowed in the summer. The newcomers were probably cattle herders who drove their beasts from one watering hole to the next.

Gradually the rainfall dwindled, the region dried up and desert took over the whole area—except for the Nile Valley. The settlers were forced to move to the fertile strip alongside the river. They arranged their lives to fit in with the pattern of the seasons there. In July the floods came, and by September the water was low enough to sow seeds. The crops ripened fast and could be harvested within a few weeks. As many as four different crops could be grown, one after the other, within a single year.

The desert on either side of the river valley gave Egypt a natural defense against invaders from the outside world. It also provided another kind of wealth—beautiful hard stones such as onyx and agate that formed naturally in the desert.

POTS AND CROCS

The Nile provided more than just fertile land. The early farmers used the black river mud to make bricks and pots. They hunted animals that sheltered in the river reeds, including water gazelles, wild ducks, and geese (others, such as crocodiles and hippopotamuses, were more dangerous). They also caught fish that were trapped in the pools left by the retreating floods.

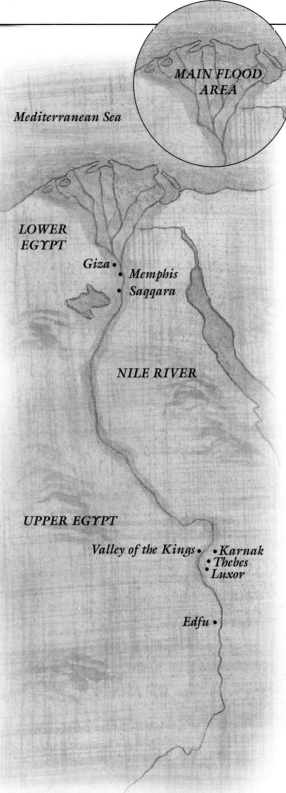

MAIN FLOOD AREA

Mediterranean Sea

LOWER EGYPT

Giza •
• *Memphis*
• *Saqqara*

NILE RIVER

UPPER EGYPT

Valley of the Kings •
• *Karnak*
• *Thebes*
• *Luxor*

Edfu •

ANNUAL FLOODING

Every year, starting in July, summer rains fell in the hills to the south of the Nile River. The rainfall drained into the river and swelled the waters of the Nile to the bursting point.

Eventually, each year, the river overflowed its banks and flooded the surrounding land. As the floodwater slowly drained away, it left behind a rich deposit of fertile mud. This damp, silty soil, warmed by the hot sun, was ideal for growing crops.

A NILOMETER
This ancient device was used to measure the annual flooding levels on the Nile.

THE OLD KINGDOM

The earliest Egyptians lived in villages and formed small communities to protect themselves against bandits. Farming was an easy task in the fertile Nile Valley, so many of the settlers also did other work. Some became craftsmen, making pottery from the river mud or carvings from bone, ivory, and stone. Some became traders, buying and selling goods with merchants along the Red Sea and the Mediterranean. Some developed one of the first kinds of writing using picture-signs called hieroglyphs.

UNITING UPPER AND LOWER

As the centuries went by, towns developed along the Nile. Different tribes formed in different areas, each with their own leaders, their own religions, and their own ways of farming. As the groups grew bigger they merged or conquered one another. By about 3200 B.C., there were two main rival groups. In the south was Upper Egypt, which stretched for most of the river's length from the rapids known as the First Cataract. In the north was Lower Egypt, which included the Delta.

WRITTEN IN STONE
Egyptian hieroglyphics were carved into stone walls and scratched into wet clay.

KING MENES

According to legend, the King of Upper Egypt at this time was named Menes. His armies defeated the troops of Lower Egypt, allowing him to unite the two regions. Carvings of the time show Menes wearing both the white crown of Upper Egypt and the red crown of Lower Egypt, symbolizing how he welded together the two parts of Egypt.

RED AND WHITE
After the time of Menes, all Egyptian kings wore a double crown of white and red.

FOUNDING MEMPHIS

There are also stories about a victorious king called Narmer, who may have been the same person as Menes. Whatever his name, this great conqueror was probably the founder of ancient Egypt. He built magnificent palaces and temples at Memphis, which lay on the border between the two regions, near present-day Cairo. From Memphis, the king kept strict control of his territory.

NARMER PALETTE
This cosmetics palette shows King Narmer defeating his enemies.

FIRST DYNASTIES

Menes was the first king of the first Egyptian dynasty. There were to be more than 30 dynasties in all, containing over 150 Egyptian kings and queens. Historians have given each dynasty a number, to help us find our way in the long history of ancient Egypt. The dynasties are in groups, covering the major periods of Egyptian history.

THE OLD KINGDOM

The first great period of ancient Egyptian history is called the "Old Kingdom." The Old Kingdom actually starts with the 3rd Dynasty (the first two belong to what is called the "Archaic Period"), and stretches for 500 years from 2686 B.C. to 2180 B.C. The Old Kingdom marks the time that Egypt reached its first peak of success, with expanding trade and the building of the massive pyramids.

PHARAOHS AND GODS

King Menes ruled his land with complete power. The Egyptians believed that Menes was a descendant of the gods. Therefore the kings who followed him must be gods too, and everyone should obey them. But the day-to-day running of the country was the job of ministers and officials. The most important of these was the vizier, who did everything from inspecting building works to judging criminals. Egypt was divided into *nomes* (districts), each governed by a local official called a "nomarch."

A GOD AMONG MEN
All the Egyptian kings were treated as gods.

THE AGE OF PYRAMIDS

Why were the pyramids built? And what were they used for? These incredible structures were built as giant tombs, to house the corpses of dead kings. Egyptians believed that every person's body had to be preserved and protected so that its soul could live on. The dead king's body had to be given the greatest and most impressive protection of all, to show the world that he had been a great and powerful man.

In ancient times, there were Seven Wonders of the World. Today, only one of these incredible Wonders has survived—the Pyramids at Giza in Egypt. These include three vast pyramids, all built during the Old Kingdom period.

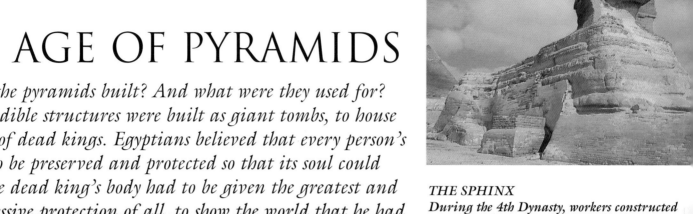

THE SPHINX

During the 4th Dynasty, workers constructed three mighty pyramids on the plain at Giza for the kings Khufu, Khefre, and Menkaure. King Khefre also ordered the carving of the huge statue of the Sphinx nearby. Before this time, Egyptian kings had been buried in flat-topped tombs called mastabas.

HOUSES FOR THE DEAD

The biggest of the Giza pyramids is the Great Pyramid, which is 759 ft. (231 m) long on each side and stands 152 ft. (94.5 m) high. It is built from more than 2.3 million blocks of stone, each weighing about 2.5 tons. Even more amazing is the accuracy of its construction. The four sides differ by no more than 8 in. (20 cm) in length, and the corners are almost exact right angles.

BUILDING BLOCKS

How did the Egyptians build these giant structures? They had no cranes, pulleys, or scaffolding, and none of the huge machines used today. Their only tools were simple ones—wooden squares, plumb lines, chisels, stone hammers, and saws made of copper.

With these tools, the builders cut through granite and basalt, some of the hardest stones in the world. Once cut, the stone blocks had to be pounded into shape with big chunks of rock held in two hands. The workers smoothed off the outer casing (made of softer limestone) with narrow copper chisels. The stone came from quarries near the Nile. The blocks were transported to the site on rafts, then hauled over land along tracks made slippery with water.

THE RIGHT SIZE
Stonemasons used simple measuring tools such as plumb lines and wooden squares to make the pyramid's stone blocks the right size and shape.

MUSCLE POWER

Huge numbers of men were needed to construct the pyramids and many men were forced to work for the king. The Great Pyramid, for example, was built in 2600 B.C. during the reign of Khufu, which lasted for about 23 years. During the construction of this pyramid, more than 300 stone blocks had to be moved and laid in position each day—that's one block every two minutes!

Only a vast workforce could have kept up this pace. Historians believe that a team of at least 25,000 men must have been working at the site at any one time. Each block needed about 20 men to move it by sled from the quarry to the pyramid, a task that took well over an hour. In addition to these workers, there were quarrymen, stonecutters, stonemasons, men who set the stones in position, metalworkers to mend tools, and carpenters to make sledges and other equipment. And a whole other team was needed simply to feed the horde of workers.

FINAL STAGES
The final stage of building the Great Pyramid was to add the outer layer of gleaming limestone. The carefully crafted blocks were added from the top down.

THE STEP PYRAMID
As Egypt grew wealthier, rulers built bigger and bigger tombs. Djoser, the second king of the 3rd Dynasty, built the first known pyramid at Saqqara. This pyramid was erected in tiers and is known as the "Step Pyramid."

EXPANDING EMPIRE

During the Old Kingdom period, Egypt grew in prosperity and power. Farmers learned better ways of controlling the annual floodwaters of the Nile. Egyptian armies kept guard on the borders of the country, defeating the troublesome "Sand Dwellers" (desert peoples) in the northeast and the wandering tribes of Palestine. The king became such a mighty figure that he could not be referred to by his name or title. Instead, people spoke of the "great house" or palace, which was pronounced per-o *in their language. From this we have the word "pharaoh."*

ORGANIZED FARMING
This Theban tomb painting c. 1400 B.C. shows cattle being herded and inspected.

KING DJOSER
Kings such as Djoser, the second king of the 3rd Dynasty, were so powerful that they were no longer referred to by name.

THE GROWTH OF TRADE

Many expeditions were sent out to trade with neighboring lands. Some went to the mysterious country of Punt, on the Red Sea, to buy incense and spices. Fleets of ships also sailed to Lebanon to fetch much-needed timber (the palm and acacia trees that grew in Egypt were of little use). Huge loads of Lebanese cedar came back to Egypt—one fleet alone consisted of 40 vessels, each crammed with trunks of cedar.

LAND OF MANY GODS

At the beginning of the Old Kingdom period, people in Egypt held differing religious beliefs. Each city and region had its own local god and system of worship. When the priests tried to organize these into some kind of national religion, the most powerful cities promoted their own "great gods" and claimed that these gods had created the universe. Memphis, for example, was the home of the creator god, Ptah.

The most important of these great gods was Re, the sun god, whose main temple was at Heliopolis, near modern Cairo. Re became the supreme royal god. Kings took the title "Son of Re." Historians believe that there was a close association between the cult of Re and the construction of skyward-pointing pyramids.

Re
the sun god

Osiris
god of the afterlife

Isis
the mother goddess

EGYPTIAN EXPORTS

Other expeditions reached Nubia, to the south of the First Cataract. Here, Egyptian traders sold oil, flax cloth, and honey, and bought in exchange, gold, ebony wood, panther skins, and hard stone for carving. In about 2250 B.C., a merchant called Harkhuf even brought back a pygmy (a member of a tribe of very short people) from Central Africa.

TRADE-OFF
Corn was another main food trading item.

CIVIL WAR

The king depended on his nobles and officials to govern his land. But after the 4th Dynasty these people began to gain more power, while the royal family grew weaker and poorer. The king had given away a lot of land to the nobles so his income was reduced. The enormous expense of building a pyramid drained the royal purse and the king also had to maintain all the tombs of his ancestors!

The nomarchs (local governors) became more independent. By the end of the 6th Dynasty, in about 2184 B.C., the nomarchs were squabbling among themselves and challenging the king's authority. Following the death of the Old Kingdom ruler, Pepi II, Egypt collapsed into civil war. The crisis was made even worse by a prolonged drought. For several years in succession, the Nile failed to rise to its normal flood level. Crops did not grow and the resulting famine was so bad that in parts of Upper Egypt people were said to have begun eating each other.

THE MIDDLE KINGDOM

The Old Kingdom came to an end in a chaos of riots and violence. Peasants abandoned their building and farming work. Tombs were destroyed, palaces were attacked, and the kings lost control of their people. It was not until about 2061 B.C. that the country was united again by a dynasty of princes from Thebes, who founded what we now call the "Middle Kingdom." Thus began a period of renewed peace and prosperity in Egypt under the rule of strong kings, which was to last until 1633 B.C.

MILITARY MIGHT
The 12th-Dynasty king Sesostris III worked hard to strengthen Egypt's defenses. He valued bravery and believed that "to retreat is wretched."

FALLEN INTO RUIN
Middle Kingdom rulers left behind nothing as grand as the Great Pyramids. Most chose to be buried beneath smaller pyramids that had elaborate labyrinths and other devices for stopping tomb-robbers. But many of the pyramids were made of mud bricks that have since crumbled away, like this mortuary temple of Rameses the Great at Luxor.

DEFENDING THE LAND

Egypt's defenses were strengthened, too. Sesostris III, who ruled from about 1860 B.C., built a line of massive brick fortresses along the southern part of the Nile to control the local population. Another string of strongholds, called the "Walls of the Rulers" guarded against attacks on the Delta region.

PROSPEROUS TIMES

This was also an age which produced much great art, including exquisite jewelry, wall paintings, and carvings. Sesostris III's son, King Amenemhet III, drained land in the marshy Faiyum region to obtain fresh land for farming. He founded new towns there and built a fine temple dedicated to Sobek, the crocodile god. Other kings enlarged the great temple to the god Amun at Karnak, near Thebes.

NEW GODS

When the Old Kingdom fell away, so did the worship of Re, the sun god. Osiris became the most popular god in Egypt, and worshipers made pilgrimages to the center of his cult at Abydos, not far from Thebes. Osiris was the god of the dead. Egyptians believed that he ruled the underworld, judging everyone equally, no matter whether they were rich or poor.

The rulers of the 12th Dynasty came from Thebes and brought with them their own royal god, Amun. This was a very different kind of god from Ptah or Osiris. He was unseen and mysterious, and so the kings were able to alter his image to suit their political purposes. Amun even traveled with the Egyptian armies on their campaigns.

WORSHIPING AMUN
The kings of the 12th Dynasty built a great temple to the god Amun at Karnak, near Thebes.

KEEPING CONTROL

The 12th-Dynasty kings tried to avoid the mistakes of earlier rulers. They limited the powers of the nomarchs, first by demanding taxes and troops from them, and then by closing their courts and taking away their privileges. The declining influence of the nomarchs is shown by a sudden absence of grand tombs after this time. In the place of the nobles, the kings encouraged a new middle class of scribes, merchants, and farmers to help them with the daily running of the government.

All the same, the kings remained very cautious. Amenemhet I warned his son not to trust anybody. He wrote him a special set of instructions, which described a dream in which he was attacked and killed by his own bodyguards. As a precaution, the 12th-Dynasty rulers allowed their heirs (usually their sons) to reign jointly with them. This reduced the risk of a palace rebellion.

READY TO WRITE
Scribes sat cross-legged with the parchment on their lap.

RULERS FROM ASIA

The long history of ancient Egypt saw the rise and fall of many dynasties. Decline, invasion, or civil war almost always followed a period of strong rule and prosperity. So it was that the powerful 12th Dynasty gave way to the very weak 13th Dynasty in about 1782 B.C. This decline lasted just over a century, during which there were 60 kings. The 14th Dynasty was even shorter and more chaotic, with 76 kings!

THE HYKSOS TAKE CHARGE

The next dynasty was a foreign one. The new rulers came from Asia, and the Egyptians called them the "Hyksos" which means "kings of foreign lands." Their reign is still a mystery. Some chronicles of ancient Egypt claim that the newcomers invaded the country, burned down the cities, destroyed the temples, and turned the people into slaves. Other historians believe that they were simply a group of Asiatic nobles who took control without a struggle from the feeble native kings.

The Hyksos built a new capital city at Avaris on the eastern part of the Nile Delta (although the site of this town has never been found). The Hyksos were not popular. Egyptians resented being ruled by foreigners and many inscriptions of the time put curses on the Asian princes and all their followers.

WAR CHARIOTS
The Hyksos went to war in horse-drawn chariots, easily defeating the Egyptian soldiers. The Egyptians learned from them and soon started to use chariots in battle too.

NEW ARMIES
Following domination by the Hyksos, the Egyptians developed organized and properly trained armies to protect their territories and expand their lands.

WARFARE AND WEAPONS

The Hyksos probably gained power because they had much greater skill in warfare than the Egyptians. They had superior weapons, including short and thin bronze swords, and strong "composite" bows made of horn and wood, which could shoot arrows at high speed. More important, they charged into battle in chariots pulled by horses, which left the ordinary footsoldiers of the Egyptian armies defenseless.

The Hyksos had another effect on military attitudes in Egypt. Humiliated by their reign, the Egyptians became determined never to be ruled by another nation again. In years to come, they were more aggressive toward their neighbors than they had ever been before and began to expand their own borders. They organized their first permanent and well-trained armies to lead these expeditions and to protect the homeland against possible invasion.

NEW TECHNOLOGY

It seems likely that the Hyksos brought stability and even helped to improve ordinary life in Egypt. During their 100-year rule, they kept to the traditional way of governing, raising taxes, repairing temples, and appointing Egyptian officials. They even took the Egyptian title "pharaoh" and wrote their names in Egyptian hieroglyphics.

New skills were introduced. Metalworkers found better methods of making bronze, which was harder than copper. Weavers began using an upright loom to make cloth, and potters developed a more efficient wheel. Farmers grew new types of vegetables and fruits, and kept humpbacked cattle, which were better able to withstand the drought and heat. Farm land was irrigated by pumping out river water using a *shaduf,* a pivoted pole with a bucket on one end and a weight on the other.

Humpbacked cattle pull a plow.

EXPELLING THE HYKSOS

While most of the Egyptians worked with the Hyksos, one part of the country stayed hostile to the Asiatic kings—Upper Egypt in the south. The rulers of Thebes led the fight—begun in about 1600 B.C.—against the Hyksos. The Hyksos army attacked and defeated the Thebans, killing their leader, Seqenenre. But his son Kamose took up the struggle. His aim, he said, was "to save Egypt and smite the Asiatics" and soon he had pushed them out of central Egypt and captured Avaris. His brother Ahmosis completed the job, driving the Hyksos out of the country by about 1570 B.C. Ahmosis went on to become the first king of the 18th Dynasty and founder of what is now called the "New Kingdom."

THE NEW KINGDOM

The New Kingdom saw ancient Egypt at the peak of its power and wealth. The long line of strong and determined rulers of the 18th Dynasty pushed the frontier as far as the River Euphrates in the east and took control of Syria and Palestine. In the south, Nubia became an Egyptian province and walled towns were built there as strongholds. Riches from these conquests poured into Egypt and were used in a glorious display of palaces and temples.

THE VALLEY OF THE KINGS
Many priceless treasures were buried with the pharaohs in their tombs, which were hidden in the cliffs west of Thebes, an area known today as the "Valley of the Kings."

THE GREAT PRINCESS

One of the earliest and most famous rulers of the New Kingdom was a woman named Hatshepsut. She was the wife of King Tuthmosis II. He died young and was succeeded by his son in 1479 B.C. But Hatshepsut pushed her son aside and became pharaoh herself. In a country that had always been ruled by men, Hatshepsut ruled for twenty years. She left behind one of the most important works of Egyptian architecture, her mortuary temple, Deir el-Bahari.

THE REIGN OF AKHENATEN

A dramatic change occurred when Amenhotep IV came to the throne in about 1367 B.C. For many years, Amun had been worshiped as the most important of Egyptian gods and a powerful organization of priests had grown up to control his cult. The new king proclaimed that there was only one god—not Amun, but Aten, the "sun disk," who had created all living things.

A NEW GOD

Amenhotep changed his name to Akhenaten, which means "it pleases Aten." He built a new city (called El-Amarna) well away from Thebes, where he went to live with his beautiful wife, Nefertiti. He encouraged his artists to show people in realistic poses rather than the traditional idealized ones, and to depict plants and animals. He suppressed the old religions, closing the rival temples and ordering Amun's name to be obliterated from monuments. This angered the priests and brought Egypt to the brink of civil war once again.

DEIR EL-BAHARI
The Mortuary Temple of Queen Hatshepsut at Thebes was a beautiful series of white courtyards and colonnades.

KING AKHENATEN
Worship of the god Aten was introduced to Egypt by King Akhenaten. Even the king's name honored the god.

TUTANKHAMUN AND THE OLD RELIGION

Akhenaten died in about 1360 B.C., still a young man. His successor was the nine-year-old Tutankhaten. His vizier, together with the priests, made sure that there was a swift return to the traditional cult of Amun. Akhenaten's brand-new city was abandoned and his temples were destroyed. The new pharaoh changed his name to Tutankhamun, in honor of the Amun. He reigned only a few years, but today he is the most famous Egyptian pharaoh, thanks to the discovery of his tomb in A.D. 1922.

RAMESES II

Akhenaten had neglected foreign affairs and Egypt's empire began to crumble. The Hittite peoples from the east invaded Syria. But among the pharaohs of the new dynasty (the 19th) were two great military leaders, Seti I and his son Rameses II. Together, they forced the Hittites to make a peace treaty and took strict control of Nubia once again.

THE EGYPTIANS AT HOME

In the New Kingdom period, there were more than three million people living in Egypt. This made it one of the most densely populated countries in the world. Most ancient Egyptians probably lived in the countryside, where they worked in the fields. Their homes were built in settlements surrounded by walls. There is little left of these small towns today. Even the great cities of ancient Egypt, such as Memphis and Thebes, have disappeared. Perhaps the best-preserved is Akhenaten's city of El-Amarna—because people only lived there for a short time!

FURNITURE

The simplest furniture, benches made of brick, were found in most homes, set against the walls for friends to sit on and chat. Other common seats were wooden stools, sometimes covered in rushes or leather. The rich and powerful furnished their homes with chairs made of fine and expensive wood, such as ebony or cedar. These were ornate and had legs carved like an animal's. Clothing and bed linen were stored in chests.

SETTLEMENTS AND HOMES

Villages and towns were built near the Nile River, but on high ground to avoid the annual flooding. Most grew up in an unplanned way, with narrow streets and houses jumbled together around the temple and other public buildings, but some villages were carefully planned. These settlements were organized for the armies of workmen who built the pyramids and other major projects. The houses were set in rows, with straight streets running down the middle.

Better-off craftsmen had homes with four or five rooms, one of which they would use as a workshop. The main rooms were all on the ground floor, grouped around a central living space. The living room walls may have been plastered and painted in bright colors. Against one wall was a raised platform, which was used as an eating area during the day and for sleeping at night. There was a staircase to the roof (often the coolest place in the house), and an outbuilding where the food was cooked.

COUNTRY VILLAS

Noblemen and wealthy government officials could afford to build large villas in the countryside. Here there was room for large gardens and outbuildings—including perhaps a swimming pool, a fish pond, an orchard, servants' quarters, and a small family temple. Egyptians loved their gardens, where they grew colorful flowers, shady trees, and fruits and vegetables.

Inside, the villa might have had as many as seventy rooms, some ornately-decorated with wall paintings or inlaid precious stones. The ceilings were lofty and supported by plastered timber pillars. Windows were usually small and high up. They were covered with lattice-work to let in the breeze but keep out the harsh sunlight—glass, of course, had not yet been invented.

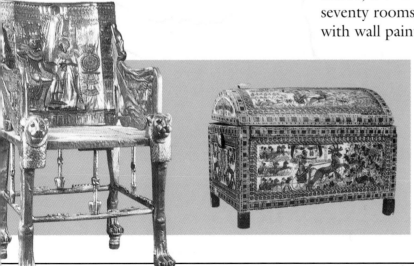

MUD HUTS
The poorest people had to make do with one-roomed huts made of mud-and-straw bricks, which they shared with their animals. Floors were simply beaten earth, though some of the bigger huts had dug-out underground cellars.

LIVES OF THE RICH
Many noblemen were buried in flat-topped tombs called mastabas, *which were often decorated with scenes from Egyptian life. This* mastaba *shows a rich nobleman sitting on an ornate wooden chair, enjoying a meal at a table in his home.*

CLOTHES AND MAKEUP

Egyptians used the simplest and cheapest material for most of their clothes. This was linen, made from the fibers of flax, a plant that was grown all over Egypt. Linen was light, strong, and easy to sew, and it could be made thick or thin to suit cool or hot weather. Weaving cloth and making clothes was the job of the women of the household. Some women even worked together in dressmaking workshops, where they sold what they produced.

CHANGING FASHIONS

Most men wore little more than a kind of kilt, which was wrapped around the waist and hung to just above the knee. It was fastened with a knot at the waist. But special groups had special clothes. The vizier wore a long, starched dress that reached up to his armpits. Priests draped leopard skins over their shoulders when performing ceremonies.

Women also wore simple clothes. Their dresses were plain white or beige, because linen was a difficult cloth to dye. The dresses covered the body from breast to ankle, with straps over the shoulders. Wealthier women had tunics decorated with elaborate needlework, and shawls or cloaks for the cooler evenings.

During the New Kingdom, fashions became more interesting and complicated. Men began to wear longer skirts, with baggy tunics and cloaks on top. Women wore pleated and fringed robes over their plain dresses. On their feet they may have worn curved and brightly-colored leather sandals—a cut above the woven grass or reed sandals worn by ordinary Egyptians. Of course, poor people often wore no shoes at all.

Egyptian broad collar

HAIR AND COSMETICS

Many Egyptian men and women had their heads shaved or their hair cut short. For special occasions they wore wigs, made from a mixture of human hair and vegetable fibers. Men and women treated their hair with scented lotions, dyed it, and even had medicines to fight baldness!

The harsh sun and dry climate meant that most people used lotions to keep their skin supple. The lotions were made of vegetable or animal fat, sometimes strongly scented with incense or myrrh (a resin taken from tree gum). Both men and women also put on eye makeup, usually a black pigment called "kohl" (a crushed mineral). Women colored their hair and nails with powdered henna, and their cheeks and lips with red ocher.

LONG HAIR
Women who kept their hair long took a lot of trouble to dress it ornately. They combed it with ivory combs and used pins and beeswax to hold curls in place.

JEWELRY

Everyone who could afford to, wore jewels. They were a protection from all kinds of harm, magical or physical. Egyptians wore small charms, or amulets, even when they were working in the fields or the workshop. The amulets were mounted on necklaces, bracelets, or rings. Doctors placed amulets of lucky stones, such as lapis lazuli or turquoise, on a patient's body to cure sickness, and priests wrapped them inside the bandages of mummified pharaohs.

Other jewelry, such as broad neck collars, was worn for show. Gold and bronze bracelets for the arms and ankles were set with gemstones and mother-of-pearl. Women kept their wigs in place with ornate headbands, sometimes decorated with live flowers.

NECK COLLARS
The most dramatic pieces of jewelry worn by the ancient Egyptians were broad collars that clasped the neck and covered the chest. These collars were made of beads or engraved metal and were sometimes so heavy that they had to have a pendant hanging down behind as a counterweight. This ornate collar was found in the tomb of Tutankhamun.

FOOD AND DRINK

Very few Egyptians went hungry. The farmland of the Nile Valley was so fertile that shortages of food were rare. Most ordinary people had a diet of beans, lentils, bread, and fish, but the wealthy enjoyed a huge variety of meats, game, wines, vegetables, and fruits. Meals were cooked on hearthstones set in an open fire or, later, in mud-brick ovens burning wood or charcoal.

BREAD AND BEER

Bread was the staple food of ancient Egypt and beer was the main drink. Women ground the wheat grains between stones until it was fine enough for flour. They made dough with yeast, milk, and salt, then left it to rise in the sun. The loaves were shaped and baked in tall brick ovens. The Egyptians made many types of bread—at least 40 names for bread, cakes, and cookies have been discovered from the New Kingdom period.

Beer was made from barley grains, which were first mixed into a dough and partly baked. This dough was then mashed up again with warm water and left to ferment before being strained off and stored in jars. Sometimes the beer was flavored with date juice or spices. Children drank the milk from cows, goats, sheep, or donkeys.

Wine was made from many different fruits including dates, figs, and grapes. Workers crushed the grapes by treading on them and left the juice to ferment in open jars. When the wine was ready, they stored it in clay jars tightly covered with rush plugs sealed with mud.

EGYPTIAN BAKERY
This tomb model shows busy bakers hard at work.

FISH AND MEAT

The Nile River was a rich source of food. Hunters killed wild birds with throwing sticks or boomerangs, or trapped them in large nets. They also collected eggs from nests. The river and the basins of floodwater were full of fish, which were caught with nets, hooked lines, or harpoons. A lot of fish was pickled with salt or dried in the sun so that it could be stored for later use.

Although the Egyptians kept cattle, they used them mainly to produce milk, pull plows, or provide sacrifices for the gods. Most meat came from other domestic animals—pigs, ducks, goats, and geese. There was also plenty of game in the surrounding rocky countryside, including gazelles, ibexes (wild goats), and antelopes. Meat was cooked by cutting it into pieces and boiling it, but sometimes whole animals were spit-roasted over an outdoor fire.

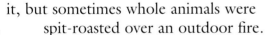

MEAL TIMES

Like us, the Egyptians enjoyed three regular meals a day. Breakfast was probably a large one, featuring bread and fruit, while the midday meal was lighter and taken as a break from the day's work. The most important meal of the day was dinner, when the family sat together. There are many paintings that show banquets held by royalty or the rich, with the diners being presented with garlands of flowers and special scented cones to wear on their heads.

Everyone ate with their fingers, carefully washing them before and during each meal with water poured from a nearby jug. At everyday meals, Egyptians did not usually sit at a table, but squatted on a large mat with their food set out in a large dish before them. Archaeologists have found many fragments of the ordinary clay bowls used for family meals.

FAMILY LIFE

Families were very important to the ancient Egyptians. The family was at the center of religious rituals. After a person died, his spirit lived on with his corpse in the tomb, as long as the tomb was tended properly. It was the job of his children and grandchildren to look after his spirit—so the more sons and daughters a person had, the better. In those days, about one baby in every three died soon after birth, but there was still an average of about five children in each family.

MARRIAGE AND CHILDREN

Men normally married women from the same place and social class, or even from the same family. Suitors from a different town or country were hard to trust. The usual age for marriage was eighteen for the husband and as young as twelve for the wife. Beforehand, the two parties drew up contracts that gave the wife the same rights as her husband in terms of owning and selling property. Divorce was a simple procedure, but the husband had to continue to support his wife.

Married couples began having children as soon as possible to carry on the family line. Women gave birth at home, under the expert eye of the local "wise woman" or midwife. Mothers breast-fed their babies for about three years—much longer than today. Wealthy couples may have hired a wet-nurse to feed and care for their children in the home. The mother chose the child's name. Egyptian names were often long and complicated and might include references to the family tree, the ruling pharaoh, and the local gods.

PARENTS AND CHILDREN
This wall mural at Thebes depicts the life of a nobleman and his family at home.

EVERYDAY WORK

There was a lot of work involved in running an Egyptian house. Women did most of this daily work. There was bread to bake, beer to brew, and grain to grind. There were clothes to wash (sometimes the job of the men), children to bathe, and walls to clean. All these tasks needed a huge amount of water, which had to be fetched from the nearest well or canal. Hygiene was always a problem, for pests and diseases could flourish in the hot climate near the Nile. There was little drainage and the only way to get rid of household trash was to throw it into the river or on to a dump as far from the house as possible. Rats, flies, and mosquitoes lived happily in such places.

WATER BOTTLE
Running an Egyptian household required lots of water. The women carried water in clay jars, which they balanced on their heads.

MUSIC

Some children learned to play musical instruments. Music was an important part of the entertainment at banquets, temple ceremonies, or just quiet nights at home. The main stringed instruments were the harp and the lute, with a sound box made of wood or a whole tortoise shell. Flutes and other wind instruments were made from reeds and metal. Dancers and listeners kept time by clapping or clicking together their wooden "clappers."

TOYS AND GAMES

Children played with all sorts of toys that we would recognize today—balls, dolls, and miniature models of hippos, crocodiles, and pigs. The balls were made of leather stuffed with straw, the dolls were made of clay, and the animals of carved wood. Many households also kept real animals as pets. The most popular pets were dogs, monkeys, baboons (kept on leashes), geese, pigeons, and cats.

As children grew older, they played more complicated games. They had mock battles with sticks and learned to swim, dance, and shoot arrows. Egyptians also played with dice and enjoyed many kinds of board games, such as senet, which was a bit like modern backgammon. The outline of the senet board could easily be scratched on to the dry earth outside the house.

WOODEN TOYS
This child's toy wooden horse dates from Roman Egypt.

CHILDREN'S TOYS
Colorful decorated rattles were made from dried-out gourds, a type of vegetable.

BOARD GAMES
Two noblewomen amuse themselves by playing chess.

SCHOOLS AND SCRIBES

Few people had formal schooling in ancient Egypt. Most children worked with their parents in the fields or the workshop as soon as they were old enough. In any case, almost all girls were kept at home where their mothers taught them the skills of housework. Only the sons of wealthy or powerful families were sent to school—and this was usually a school for scribes. Anyone who wanted to work as a government official had to be able to read and write.

LEARNING TO BE A SCRIBE

Boys began school when they were five. This must have been dull, because the pupils seem to have spent most of their time reciting lessons and copying out simple texts. They picked up the basic style and learned the different signs. At ten, the boys went on to scribal school, which was usually run by the priests of a temple. The teachers were very strict and beat anyone who was lazy or behaved badly.

ANCIENT WRITING
A page of hieroglyphics from **The Book of the Dead,** *written on paper-like papyrus scrolls.*

LIFE AS A WRITER
Statue of a scribe from the 5th Dynasty. As a scribe, you could spend all day writing—in particular, keeping records on tomb walls.

SPECIALIZED SKILLS

The pupils practiced their writing on plain tablets made of wood or on pieces of old clay pots called *ostraca*. Mistakes could easily be rubbed out or washed off. When they left school at last, the boys still had much to learn. They went to work for a master scribe, or attended a government, religious, or army college where they learned specialty skills. Now they were in the top grade of Egyptian workers. As an old Egyptian text said: "No scribe is short of food or of riches from the palace."

SCROLLS, SYMBOLS, AND SOUNDS

Nearly all Egyptian documents, from records to prayers, were written down by the scribes on scrolls made of papyrus (an early kind of paper made from reeds). Instead of letters, the scribes used hieroglyphics, a system of symbols that conveyed different sounds and ideas. Learning to write was a mammoth task, because there were more than eight hundred separate symbols to memorize.

The earliest hieroglyphics were simple pictures of objects that Egyptians could easily recognize, such as a cat, a bird, or a snake. But scribes also had to be able to write about more complex things—about ideas, or about abstract actions like thinking, or planning, or loving. Another kind of hieroglyphic sign was developed to show these kinds of ideas, using the sound of each symbol. For example, in Egyptian the word for "eye" was pronounced *ir* and the word for "mouth" was pronounced *ro*. By putting together the signs for sounds like these, the scribes could build up many new words.

SCRIBES AT WORK

Scribes wrote on papyrus, a very important material, for it was strong and long-lasting, and could be rolled up without cracking. The scribe kept his colors and tools in a wooden box, which he placed beside him. Inside the box was a palette, or board, with little hollows to store the different pigments. The scribe used pens made of reed with the ends frayed to act like brushes.

First, the scribe dipped the brush in a pot of water to moisten it. Then he rubbed the wet brush onto one of the dry, colored pigments.

READING THE HIEROGLYPHIC ALPHABET

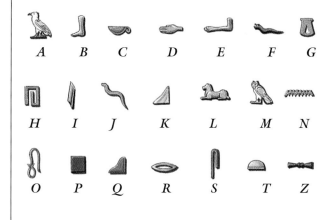

A B C D E F G

H I J K L M N

O P Q R S T Z

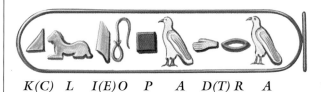

K(C) L I(E)O P A D(T)R A

The hieroglyphic alphabet consisted of more than eight hundred different signs. Many were pictures of animals, people, or objects. Hieroglyphs might be written from left to right, right to left, top to bottom, or bottom to top. Still, Egyptians knew which way to read them. If the symbols for people or animals faced left, the Egyptians read from left to right. If they faced right, they read from right to left.

MAKING A LIVING

*Society in ancient Egypt was built up like a pyramid.
The pharaoh was at the top, all-powerful, and very rich.
Just below him were the government officials and priests.
At the very bottom were the huge numbers of slaves
(often prisoners of war), peasant laborers, and unpaid
servants. They were uneducated and did all the worst jobs
in the homes and fields. In between were the builders,
farmers, craftsmen, merchants, and scribes. Everyone
owed work or duty to the person above them.*

FARMERS

As soon as the yearly floodwaters had gone
down, men moved across the black-silted
fields. They repaired the ditches and
channels, cleared away weeds, and
broke up the soil with hoes. Plows
pulled by oxen or donkeys were
used to gouge out furrows.
Following them were the sowers,
scattering seed by hand. The
growing crops were irrigated by
directing water from the river or
flood basins along the ditches and
into the fields.

Tax officials
measured the crop,
to decide how much
tax each farmer
would have to pay.
Then came the
harvest. The farmer
cut his maize and
spread the ears out on
the ground, where

MAIZE

they were trampled by oxen to
break off the husks. Then
the farmer winnowed his
maize—tossing it in the air
with wooden fans so that
the lighter husks blew away.
The grain was stored in silos
made of mud bricks. Other
important crops included figs,
grapes, pomegranates, and dates.
Farmers also kept bees for
honey, the only kind of
sweetener known at the time.

CARGO SHIPS
Stone and other heavy cargo were transported by boat along the Nile.

HUNTERS OF THE MARSHES

The marshes along the banks of the Nile provided work for many people. There were many wild plants to be gathered—water flowers and reeds for making ropes, mats, and baskets, and papyrus for making paper or even small boats. Workers pulled up bundles of papyrus and stripped away the outer bark before cutting the stem into strips. These strips were set in crisscross layers and then hammered with a mallet until they were flat and bonded together.

There were many wild birds and fish to hunt along the Nile. Hunters lured the birds into a double net, which sprang shut when ropes were pulled. The best birds were fattened up in the poultry yard, while the others were killed immediately for the table. The hunters also used nets for fishing. They lowered a net to the bottom of the river, weighed down with stones, then pulled it up quickly to snare the fish.

CRAFTSMEN

Artists and craftsmen flourished in the prosperous setting of the Nile Valley. Over the centuries they developed amazing skills using only simple materials and tools. Clay was used to make everyday objects such as bowls and cups, but stone was used to make great ornaments. Stoneworkers cut the stone into blocks with saws and then carved them to shape with chisels. It must have taken enormous patience to work with very hard stones like alabaster.

PAINTERS AND CARPENTERS

Carpenters used imported wood from countries such as Phoenicia and Lebanon. They were highly skilled and crafted many everyday items—from furniture to boats. Their most prized work was the making of grand coffins for tombs and the carving of statues of gods for the temples. These were often covered in gold leaf or inlaid with patterns of ebony and ivory.

Painters decorated the walls of tombs and temples with pictures of the next world, which would come alive for the spirits of the dead. They made their colors from minerals and added glue or egg to make the paint stick to the walls. Their brushes were sticks of wood that had been soaked in water to loosen the fibers at the tip.

33

ANCIENT EGYPTIAN GODS

The ancient Egyptians saw the world in a very different way from us. They believed that Egypt itself lay at the center, a flat mound in the middle of the waters of Nun, the underworld. The Nile River flowed from these life giving waters and every morning the Sun rose out of them. A scarab beetle pushed the Sun across the sky as if it were a ball of dung. This world was watched over by a network of gods. They varied between regions and changed their names and roles over the centuries, but formed the most important part of an Egyptian's life.

HORUS
This statue of the falcon god, Horus, stands in the Temple of Edfu. The god Horus came to represent the spirit of the pharaoh.

HOW THE WORLD WAS MADE

The Egyptians had many different stories about the creation of the world. One of these stories told of Atum, the creator god, who caused the mound of earth to rise out of the dark, endless ocean of Nun. He then made two new gods—one for the air and one for the water. They in turn gave birth to Geb, the god of the earth, and Nut, the goddess of the sky.

Another story describes how Atum left a gigantic egg on the mound. When the egg hatched, the Sun emerged from inside. Atum later became merged with Re, the sun god. Egyptians believed that Atum-Re traveled across the sky each day, going down into the dark underworld at night.

OSIRIS AND ISIS

Geb and Nut had four children, including Osiris the well-loved god of farmers and winemakers, and Seth, who ruled the desert and created storms. The evil Seth killed his brother Osiris, chopped his body into pieces and scattered them across the land. But, their sister Isis found all the pieces, and used her magic powers to put Osiris together again. Isis and Osiris then had a son called Horus. When he grew up, Horus attacked Seth, eager to avenge his father's death. After a long conflict, the senior gods banished Seth. Osiris became ruler of the underworld and god of the dead, while Horus became the spirit of the Egyptian monarch. Each pharaoh took on the earthly form of Horus while he lived. When a pharaoh died, he was then transformed into Osiris.

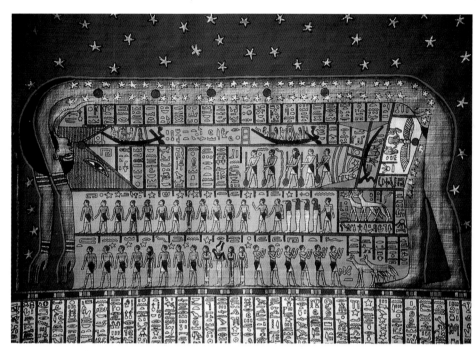

GODDESS OF THE SKY
This picture shows Nut, goddess of the sky, painted blue and covered in stars, arching over her brother the earth.

ANUBIS
Protector of the dead.

GODS AND ANIMALS

Some of the gods were identified with animals or special symbols. Many paintings show Horus with the head of a falcon, while Anubis (protector of the dead) is shown with a jackal's head. Another type of dog-god was Wepwawet, called the "Opener of the Ways," whose head was depicted on the flags that Egyptian kings carried when they went into battle.

Hathor, goddess of music and love, wore cow horns on her head, and Sekhmet, goddess of war and fire, had the head of a lioness. There were also gods for every aspect of an Egyptian's life, including Bes, the dwarf god of the family, and Taweret, the hippopotamus goddess who protected pregnant women.

35

THE GOD KINGS

All Egyptians looked up to their pharaoh as the most important person in the land. The welfare of the whole country was in his hands. One text reads: "His eyes probe every being. He shines on Egypt more brightly than the sun disk. He makes things greener than the great flood. He fills Egypt with strength and life." And he was even more powerful than that—in fact, he was a god from the moment he was born. During the Old Kingdom, kings were seen as the sons of Re. By the time of the New Kingdom, the state god had changed and kings were now regarded as the sons of Amun.

HORUS
The Egyptians believed that the pharaoh was the living god, Horus, on Earth. Horus was usually shown as a falcon, or falcon-headed. The eye of Horus was believed to be a lucky amulet with the power to protect everything behind it.

GIFTS FOR THE GODS
This wall carving shows Rameses II kneeling down to present gifts to the god Amun-Re, who is seated. This image was carved in a wall that forms part of the Karnak Temple in Thebes.

RITUALS AND CEREMONIES

The king had huge power, but he also had duties. He protected his people and appeared before them in a series of ceremonies throughout the year. Some of these ceremonies were connected with the annual flooding of the Nile River—a vital moment in the Egyptian calendar. The king dug the first spadeful of soil to open up irrigation canals and performed rituals which encouraged the river to rise. At other times he laid foundation stones for new temples or simply showed himself to his subjects, traveling by royal barge up the Nile.

Even kings grow old and weak, but the pharaoh had to seem all-powerful. After he had reigned for about thirty years, the king had to take part in a special ritual to renew his magical strength. First of all, priests buried a statue of the "old" king. Then the "new" king made a tour of major sacred sites, where he demonstrated his refreshed powers in running, archery, and other athletic exercises.

CROWN AND SCEPTER

The king also had a special costume. Instead of the common loincloth, he wore a pleated apron with a triangular front. On his head, he generally placed a striped cloth called the *nemes*, which hung down on either side of his face (like the nemes on the famous death mask of Tutankhamun). At other times, he wore the double crown—the Red Crown of Lower Egypt with its strange coil and the bulbous White Crown of Upper Egypt.

A pharaoh had to carry several symbols of his majesty. On his headdress was a *diadem* in the shape of a cobra, ready to spit deadly defiance at his enemies. On his chin was a false beard, a sign of his masculine strength. Attached to his waist was a bull's tail, which was another token of his great power. In his hands, the king held the two symbols of his office—a long stick shaped like a shepherd's crook and a flail which he could also use to swat away pesky flies).

MARRIAGE

As the pharaoh was a god, he could not take an ordinary mortal to be his queen. So it became the custom for kings to marry someone from his own family—someone who was a close blood relative and thus partly connected to the gods. Many kings married several wives, including their sisters or half-sisters, or even, sometimes, one of their own daughters.

BEAUTY QUEEN
Nefertiti, the wife of King Akhenaten (1352–1336 B.C.) was famous for her outstanding beauty.

TUTANKHAMUN
This famous pharaoh was buried in three coffins, that fitted inside each other like Russian dolls. The coffins were exquisitely decorated and showed the young pharaoh holding his crook and flail.

PREPARING FOR DEATH

A king often spent a large part of his reign preparing for his death. He planned and supervised the building of a suitably grand tomb, such as a pyramid or (during the New Kingdom) a secret spot in the Valley of the Kings. The Egyptians believed that death was just the beginning of eternal life. The spirit of the dead pharaoh would stay attached to his body and live on in the tomb, still watching over the land and its people.

37

PYRAMID BURIAL

When a king died, it was a national disaster for the Egyptians. They had suddenly lost their protector. There was only one way to overcome this crisis. The king's corpse had to be ushered into the underworld with a series of grand and mysterious rituals. The tomb would become his new home and a center of worship dedicated to his memory. In this way, the old king could live on as a god in the underworld and in his tomb, while a new pharaoh took his place.

JOURNEY TO THE TOMB

During the period of the Old Kingdom and for much of the Middle Kingdom, most royal tombs took the form of pyramids. Attendants wrapped the king's body in cloth and laid it on a funeral barge. Priests stood protectively around the corpse as the barge traveled across the river and up a specially-built canal to the site of the pyramid itself. The barge traveled from east to west, following the course of the sun as it sets into the Kingdom of the Dead.

INTO THE VALLEY TEMPLE

The massive pyramid dominated the tomb complex, which also contained temples, courtyards, and the smaller tombs of officials and courtiers, called *mastabas*. The royal corpse would be unloaded at a stone landing stage and then carried into the lowest temple, called the valley temple.

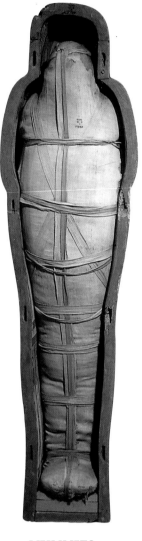

MUMMIES
The mummy of this Theban princess was wrapped in its final shroud, then placed in a beautiful, painted mummy case.

IN PROCESSION
The king's body was carried solemnly from the barge to the temple.

*RAMESES II
Mummification
has preserved this
king's body for
over 3,000 years.*

*IN STORAGE
The mummy's
internal organs
were removed
and stored in
canopic jars.*

*SECRET
PASSAGES
Inside the Great
Pyramid at Giza.*

MUMMIFICATION

The next stage was to preserve the body by embalming (or "mummifying") it. Egyptians believed that when a person died, they released a cloud of spirits, including the life force (the *ka*) and the person's own character (the *ba*). These two spirits could only live on if the dead body was well-preserved, for the *ka* stayed with the body, while the *ba* made a journey into the underworld every day. If the corpse decayed, the *ba* would have nowhere to return to at night.

PRESERVED IN PEACE

Inside the valley temple, the embalmers washed the king's body and then prepared it for burial. They removed the lungs, liver, and other organs, wrapped them, and placed them in decorated jars called "canopic jars." They then dried the body completely, using a salt called *natron*, and stuffed it with linen and spices. Next they anointed it with preserving oils and lotions. Finally, the corpse was carefully wrapped in many feet of linen bandage. Priests placed jewels and amulets in the folds of the linen.

THE HEART OF THE PYRAMID

After seventy days, bearers placed the body in a wooden coffin, which they lifted onto a sled. They pulled the sled up a long sloping causeway to the second, or funerary, temple. Here the priests performed their ceremony, making offerings of food and drink to the gods, and reciting funeral texts. Next, the bearers hauled the coffin out of the temple and into the pyramid, followed by a long procession of priests, relatives, and mourners.

They went through a maze of dark, narrow tunnels and into a room in the heart of the huge pyramid, the funeral chamber. The first coffin was placed inside a second coffin, carved from solid stone. The priests read the final words and left papyrus texts with magic spells to help the spirit reach the underworld safely. The coffin was surrounded with food, drink, personal possessions, and treasures—everything the dead person would need in the afterlife. Then everyone left and the bearers sealed up the door so that no one could ever enter the tomb again.

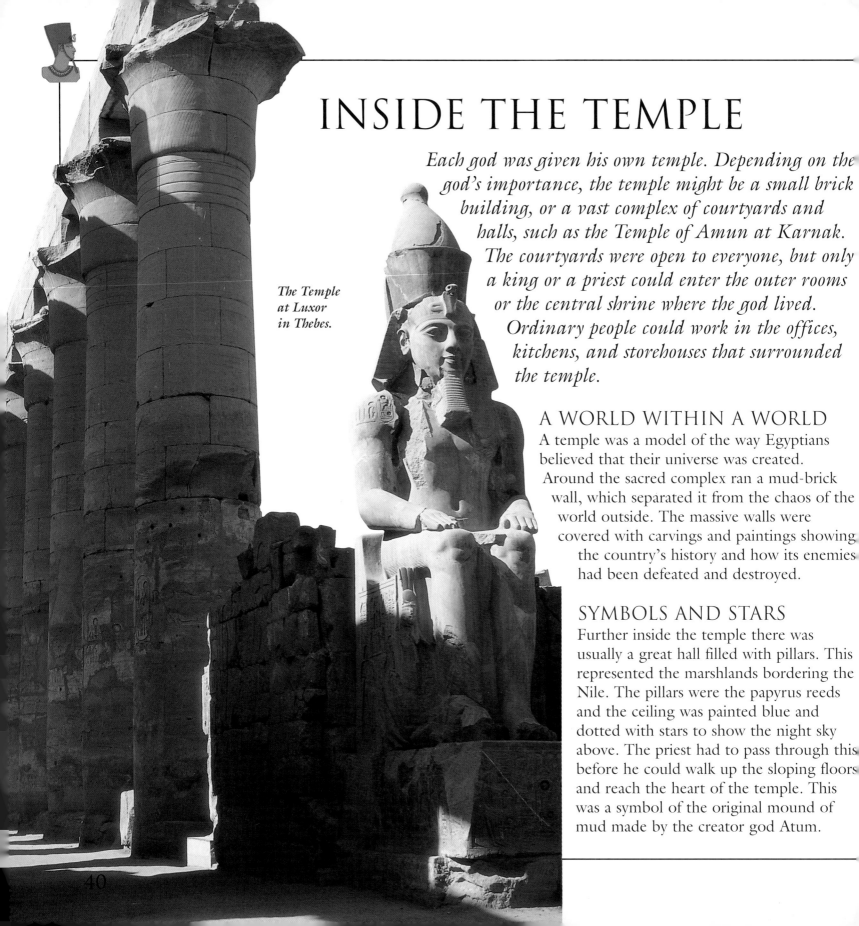

INSIDE THE TEMPLE

Each god was given his own temple. Depending on the god's importance, the temple might be a small brick building, or a vast complex of courtyards and halls, such as the Temple of Amun at Karnak. The courtyards were open to everyone, but only a king or a priest could enter the outer rooms or the central shrine where the god lived. Ordinary people could work in the offices, kitchens, and storehouses that surrounded the temple.

The Temple at Luxor in Thebes.

A WORLD WITHIN A WORLD

A temple was a model of the way Egyptians believed that their universe was created. Around the sacred complex ran a mud-brick wall, which separated it from the chaos of the world outside. The massive walls were covered with carvings and paintings showing the country's history and how its enemies had been defeated and destroyed.

SYMBOLS AND STARS

Further inside the temple there was usually a great hall filled with pillars. This represented the marshlands bordering the Nile. The pillars were the papyrus reeds and the ceiling was painted blue and dotted with stars to show the night sky above. The priest had to pass through this before he could walk up the sloping floors and reach the heart of the temple. This was a symbol of the original mound of mud made by the creator god Atum.

40

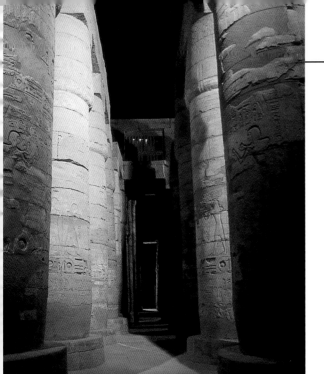

THE TEMPLE OF KARNAK
Columns from the Temple of Karnak in Thebes. On the west bank of the Nile is the magnificent temple of Hatshepsut, while on the east bank are the temples of Luxor and Karnak.

THE TEMPLES AT THEBES

The greatest of the ancient Egyptian temples were built at Thebes. This city was the nation's capital for long periods and became the center for the worship of Amun and other important gods. The hot, dry climate of the region has helped to preserve its wonderful temples and tombs better than those that were built in the damper north.

LOCAL SHRINES

Ordinary Egyptians could not go into the central sanctuaries of the great temples. Instead, they worshiped at much smaller local shrines. They went there to say prayers, or to present an offering of food or a *stele*. This was a small clay slab, inscribed with a prayer or a letter to a dead relative, a picture of the god—and also, sometimes, a line of ears to make sure that the message was heard!

Most people also kept religious items in their homes. They placed busts of their ancestors in niches (hollow spaces) in the walls of their living rooms, as well as images of household gods such as Bes and Taweret. Wealthy Egyptians with large homes even had small temples or shrines built within their grounds.

CULT COLLECTION

The cult center at Karnak was the wealthiest and most ambitious of all. It was really a collection of temples and the biggest of these was the Great Temple of Amun—one of the largest religious structures ever built. Founded by rulers during the Middle Kingdom in about 1990 B.C., it was massively extended and redecorated under the New Kingdom.

An avenue of carved sphinxes leads to a series of halls, separated by *pylons*, or gateways. The famous hypostyle hall lies between the second and third pylons. Its roof of stone slabs is held up by 134 stone columns, most of which are carved in the shape of papyrus plants. At the very center of the building is the sanctuary where Amun lived.

A LINE OF LIONS
This photograph of the Avenue of Sphinxes at Karnak in Thebes was taken in 1878.

BEING A PRIEST

The pharaoh was the high priest of all the temples in Egypt, for he was a god and had a direct link with the other gods. The vizier and the prophets and officials closest to the king were the senior priests. Below them were the ordinary priests, who performed the religious ceremonies that took place every day throughout the land. Egyptians believed that these rituals were vital for peace and order in the world. If the gods were properly worshiped and fed, they would look after people on Earth.

SENIOR PRIESTS
These sculptures date from the reign of Amenemhat III. It is thought they are senior priests, probably a vizier and a regional govenor.

THE DAILY RITUAL

Each morning and evening the high priest, wearing his leopard-skin ceremonial cloak, broke the seal on the door of the inner shrine. Inside, he bowed before the bronze or gold statue of the god. The god was greeted with hymns and prayers and the statue was washed, dressed with perfumed oils, and fitted with clothing and a crown. The temple musicians played *sistrums*, sacred musical instruments like metal rattles.

Next the god was fed to give him energy for the new day. Egyptians believed that gods needed food and drink, just as ordinary mortals did. The priests laid offerings of food and wine in front of the statue. Later, they removed these offerings—perhaps for their own meals! The high priest walked out of the shrine backward, brushing away his footprints as he went, then shut the door and put back the seal.

***RITES BEFORE
THE TOMB***
*This is an illustration
from the* **Book of the
Dead of Hunefer,** *from
the 19th Dynasty.*

*The centerpiece of this
scene shows the mummy
of Hunefer, supported by
the god Anubis, or a
priest wearing a jackal
mask. Hunefer's wife
and daughter mourn,
and three priests
perform rituals. The
two priests with white
sashes are carrying out
the "Opening of the
Mouth" ritual.*

GODS ON TOUR

There were many religious festivals during the year, when the god was taken from his shrine and placed in a special cabin, decorated with gold, silver, or precious stone. Priests carried the cabin on their shoulders into the outer courtyards. Sometimes, the god was taken out of the temple complex and carried to visit other gods.

This happened at the major festivals, celebrating events such as the coming of the floods or the harvest, and was watched by vast crowds of people. At the Feast of Opet, for example, the image of Amun traveled from his temple at Karnak by river barge to the nearby temple at Luxor, where there was another image of the same god. This was a riotous holiday, with music bands, dancing girls, banquets, and sacrifices.

LIFE AS A PRIEST

A priest lived modestly, only eating certain foods and bathing at least twice a day to make sure he was completely clean and pure. He shaved his entire body regularly, and normally wore simple, white linen clothes. Priests worked in teams. These teams took charge of the temple rituals for one month before handing over to the next team. Besides these teams of priests, there were great numbers of minor priests who looked after the estates, which were often enormous. During the reign of Rameses III, the Theban temples owned fifty-six entire towns and four hundred thousand cattle!

During the period of the Old Kingdom, priests were carefully selected. They had to be good-looking, healthy, and clever—they had to be able to read the many texts involved in the temple rituals throughout the year. As the priesthood grew more powerful, huge numbers of unsuitable people became priests. The wealth and plentiful food of the temples attracted many recruits.

FALSE DOORS
*This image shows a limestone false door to the
tomb of the high priest, Ptahshepses, from the 5th
Dynasty. He was the high priest of Ptah.*

VALLEY OF THE KINGS

The pyramids, with their royal ghosts and sumptuous grave goods, remained sealed up for many centuries. But eventually the magic of the tomb faded and robbers broke in to ransack the treasures. During the New Kingdom period, King Amenophis I decided that he should be buried in a less obvious place—somewhere hidden from thieving eyes. He chose a remote valley near Thebes on the west bank of the Nile, above which loomed a pyramid-shaped cliff. Many other monarchs followed his example. Today, this area is known as the "Valley of the Kings."

TUNNEL TOMBS

Instead of building a grand memorial above ground, the New Kingdom rulers had their tombs dug down into the rock of the valley, with the entrance carefully concealed. From here, a series of long corridors ran deep underground, full of confusing twists and turns. They passed through several halls before reaching the burial chamber, a dark and silent room which must have seemed an exact model of the underworld. The walls of the passage were painted with scenes showing the king being transformed into a god.

Over the next five centuries, all the Egyptian pharaohs were buried here. More than sixty of them have been discovered. These later tombs were some of the largest man-made caverns ever constructed. The wives of the kings were placed in tombs in a separate site to the south, which is known as the "Valley of the Queens."

TREASURES
This beautiful statue (left) and this jeweled breastplate (right) were among the treasures discovered in the tomb of Tutankhamun, in the Valley of the Kings.

BRACELETS
These scarab bracelets from Tutankhamun's tomb were made from gold and inset with semiprecious jewels.

DESERT TOMBS
This desolate burial site is known as the Valley of the Kings. More than sixty pharaohs were buried here.

TRICKS AND TRAPS

The burial chambers were filled with precious objects such as beautiful clothes and perfumes, gold-plated statues and weapons, and ornaments carved from alabaster. The builders knew that robbers would try to get inside so they added many tricks and booby traps to keep them out.

MASTERS OF DISGUISE

Some of the corridors led to blank walls. Secret entrances to burial chambers were concealed in ceilings. Important doorways were hidden in unexpected places or disguised with coats of plaster to look like the walls. Deep pits were dug for the robbers to fall into and mounds of sand were suspended that would collapse on top of any intruder who moved a certain stone slab. But for all their careful planning, the pharaohs could not keep their secrets forever. In the end the robbers forced their way in, stole what they could sell, and often smashed the rest.

THE SECRET VILLAGE

The pharaohs did not want their laborers to tell everyone about the Valley of Kings and what was buried there. So a special village was built, well away from the other communities. The workers and their families were kept isolated from the outside world.

This village was called Deir el-Medina. The king paid the workers with water and food which had to be carried in by teams of donkeys. Teams of fishermen caught them fish from the Nile, while professional washerwomen did their laundry. The gangs of builders worked for a ten-day stint, spending the night in shelters near the tomb sites before going home to their families. The secret village flourished for about four hundred years, with fathers handing on their skilled and valuable jobs to their sons.

TOMB RAIDERS
This jumble of treasures, found in Tutankhamun's tomb, was probably abandoned by startled robbers.

NEW KINGDOM CONQUESTS

Whenever Egypt grew weak, she became vulnerable to invasion from her neighboring countries. The Libyans, the Nubians, and the Hittites all seized parts of Egyptian territory when the opportunity arose. During the 19th Dynasty, the kings Seti I and Rameses II showed that their armies could still be a powerful force. Rameses fought a bloody but indecisive battle against the Hittites at Kadesh in about 1275 B.C. and was able to take back control of much of Syria. After this, however, Egypt declined again. The rulers of the 20th Dynasty had to face severe money troubles as well as a new set of invaders.

INVADING ARMIES
This model shows Nubian soldiers advancing against Egyptian forces.

THE COLLAPSE OF AN EMPIRE

Rameses III was the last of the great Egyptian rulers. His reign ended in 1158 B.C. when historians think he may have been murdered. Gradually, Egypt lost her territories in Asia. Tomb robbers began breaking into the royal tombs at Thebes and stole many hidden riches. In the centuries that followed the end of the New Kingdom, there was a series of invasions.

First, a Libyan dynasty established itself at Bubastis on the Nile Delta. Then, after a period of civil war, Nubian kings took control of Thebes and Memphis. In 663 B.C., the Assyrians advanced into Egypt and destroyed the Egyptian army, sacking Thebes and looting its great treasures. The Assyrians were followed by the Babylonians and, later, by the Persians, who won a decisive victory at Pelusium in 525 B.C. The Persians ruled Egypt for nearly two hundred years.

THE EGYPTIAN ARMY AND NAVY

The shock of the invasion by the Hyksos at the end of the Middle Kingdom had brought a new, warlike spirit to the country. To guard against further invasion, the Egyptians built up an efficient and well-equipped army. They began using war chariots. While a charioteer drove, a soldier behind was able to shoot arrows at the enemy. The chariots were backed up by foot soldiers carrying spears, battleaxes, or bronze swords. In later years, the Egyptians also built up a navy to deal with the attacks of the Sea Peoples. In a great sea battle at the mouth of the Nile, Rameses III equipped his ships with battering rams that sank many of the enemy's boats. His ships were filled with archers, who shot showers of arrows into the invaders.

RAMESES THE GREAT
This painted relief depicts Rameses II (1304–1237 B.C.) with Nubian prisoners.

THE SEA PEOPLES

In about 1200 B.C. bands of fierce warriors, known as the Sea Peoples, began raiding the eastern borders of Egypt. Some were pirates, who attacked towns and ships off the Egyptian coast. Others were wandering groups who had been forced to migrate westward because of famine in their native lands. The Sea Peoples joined forces with the Libyans and attacked the Nile Delta from the west. Rameses managed to stop them landing in Egypt and destroyed their fleet in about 1186 B.C. The Sea Peoples retreated and began colonizing Palestine and the islands of the Mediterranean.

PRISONERS OF WAR
This wall carving at Abu Simbel shows defeated enemy soldiers, who were enslaved and brought home by the victorious Egyptians.

ALEXANDER THE GREAT

For nearly two hundred years, the Persians ruled Egypt. During that time they were driven out for a short period, but always regained control. The Persian king appointed a satrap, or governor, to rule the country in his name, collecting taxes and passing laws. Many foreigners came to live in Egypt—not only Persians but also Greeks from across the Mediterranean. Then, in 332 B.C. an entire Greek army arrived, led by Alexander the Great, the all-conquering king of Macedonia in Greece. The Persians knew that they could not resist such a mighty force and so they quickly surrendered.

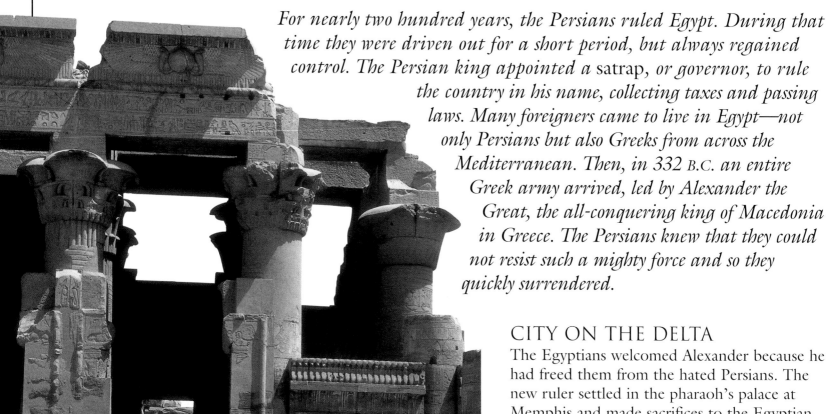

NEW TEMPLES
This photograph shows the Hellenistic temple at Kom Ombo, Egypt.

CITY ON THE DELTA

The Egyptians welcomed Alexander because he had freed them from the hated Persians. The new ruler settled in the pharaoh's palace at Memphis and made sacrifices to the Egyptian gods. Soon after this, he sailed to the mouth of the Nile, where he was determined to found a new city and establish his power over the land.

The site he chose was a perfect one, with a mild climate and a sheltered harbor. There was easy access to the trade routes of the Mediterranean and to the fertile farmlands further up the Nile. Alexander even showed where the city boundaries should go. Taking flour from his soldiers' packs, he sprinkled lines on the ground to show the position of the city walls. The site, soon called Alexandria, grew into one of the world's great cities.

***ALEXANDER THE GREAT** This powerful warrior ruled Egypt from 332 B.C. to 323 B.C.*

DESERT PILGRIMAGE

A few weeks after his trip up the Nile, Alexander made a second, and more mysterious, journey. This took him south and west through the hot desert to a small town on Egypt's borders. Here at Siwah was a shrine to the great god, Amun, in which there was an oracle (a spirit which could foretell the future).

After a solemn ceremony, Alexander went into the shrine to speak to the oracle alone. Some historians believe that he asked whether he would succeed in conquering the Persian Empire, and that the god replied that he would conquer the entire world! This story was probably made up later. All the same, Alexander's pilgrimage to Siwah showed the Egyptians that he respected their gods.

***THE PHAROS** This 18th-century picture shows the great lighthouse (Pharos) of Alexandria, which was built in 280 B.C.*

AFTER ALEXANDER

Alexander spent very little time in Egypt. He had many more amazing deeds to perform—the final defeat of the Persians, the march up into the icy mountains of Afghanistan, and the conquest of northern India. He died young from an illness in 323 B.C. but he had already built up the biggest empire ever known.

Alexander's empire fell apart after his death, yet the dynasty he established in Egypt ruled for another three hundred years. They were descended from a Macedonian soldier called Ptolemy, who buried the emperor's body at Alexandria and then declared himself King of Egypt. He was followed by a long line of rulers, most of whom were called Ptolemy. During this period, Macedonian and Greek soldiers struggled to maintain control of the land.

Greek settlers began to replace Egyptians in the more powerful positions in the country. Alexandria became a center for Greek culture and learning, with the very first museum and the biggest library in the world. A vast lighthouse, the Pharos, was built on an island outside the harbor. It was more than 396 ft. (120 m) high and became famous as one of the Seven Wonders of the World.

ROMAN EGYPT AND AFTER

The Ptolemies had a hard time clinging to power in Egypt. In about 67 B.C., a force of native Egyptians, tired of foreign domination, expelled Ptolemy XII from the country. He turned to Rome for help. Roman power was growing rapidly under the joint rule of three men (the Triumvirate)—among them Julius Caesar. They gladly sent troops to restore the king to his throne. Egypt passed into the hands of another master and became a monarchy protected by Rome.

CLEOPATRA

When the king died in 51 B.C. his son, Ptolemy XIII, became ruler, but he was a weak and hesitant monarch and soon his bolder and stronger sister took control. Her name was Cleopatra, and she was the most famous of all the ancient Egyptians. Cleopatra dreamed of regaining control of Egypt's lost territories and of sharing in the central power at Rome.

Her chance came in 48 B.C., when Julius Caesar arrived in Alexandria. Using her charm and intelligence, she persuaded the old soldier to make an alliance with her against her enemies. Caesar defeated her opponents and gave her a sumptuous villa near Rome. The pair had a son, who ruled jointly with his mother as Ptolemy XV.

ANTONY AND CLEOPATRA

Caesar was murdered in 44 B.C., but Cleopatra soon found another powerful ally, Mark Antony, one of the new Roman leaders. They became lovers, but the affair created political arguments, then war against Rome. The Roman fleet defeated the Egyptians at the Battle of Actium in 31 B.C. Antony and Cleopatra committed suicide. Cleopatra died from a snake bite—Egyptians believed snakes to be agents of the god Amun.

RULED FROM ROME

After the death of Cleopatra, Romans took complete charge of Egypt. They saw their new prize as a rich land to be squeezed dry. With typical efficiency they cleared out neglected irrigation ditches and revived farming. They needed the huge grain crops of the Nile Valley to feed the people of Rome—and the Egyptians had what was left over. What is more, the Roman system of taxation was even harsher than that of the old pharaohs, and the native Egyptians grew steadily poorer.

The final blow fell in A.D. 383, by which time much of the Roman Empire had become Christian. The Emperor Theodosius ordered that all pagan (non-Christian) temples should be closed down. The statues of the old gods were torn from their sanctuaries and chopped to pieces. People who followed pagan ways were persecuted and even killed. The civilization of the ancient Egyptians died along with their religion.

Julius Caesar

MUSLIM CONQUERORS

Egypt was now officially a Christian country. Churches and monasteries were built on new sites and many small communities grew up in the deserts near the Nile. The Christians of Egypt even had their own special name—the Copts. Even after the Roman Empire finally collapsed during the fifth century A.D., the new religion continued to flourish. A cathedral was built at Hermopolis, a place that Christians revered because they believed that Jesus and his family had stayed there when they fled into Egypt.

But yet another enormous change was on the way. In A.D. 639 Arab followers of the new Islamic religion burst out of Syria and invaded Egypt. Within three years they had captured Alexandria and established a military stronghold in Cairo. The country was slowly transformed into an important part of the Islamic Empire and Islamic culture replaced the Christian one. Egyptians began to speak Arabic and to produce some of the greatest masterpieces of Islamic art and architecture.

ANTONY AND CLEOPATRA
This 19th-century painting by Sir Lawrence Alma-Tadema depicts a meeting between Mark Antony and Cleopatra. The Roman boat is being rowed by Roman soldiers. Cleopatra is dressed in fine leopard-skin robes.

LOST AND FOUND

Egypt now entered a millennium of neglect. Over the centuries the ruins of its ancient civilization were pillaged. People pulled down temples to use the old stone for building houses. Robbers looted tombs and palaces of their treasures. Mummified bodies were taken out, pulled to pieces, and sold—as a magical ingredient in medicine! The Egyptian religion disappeared and the meaning of the hieroglyphic writing and other scripts was lost.

THE ROSETTA STONE

The rediscovery of ancient Egypt really began in 1798. The French leader Napoleon led an army from the Nile Delta into Upper Egypt. Napoleon brought with him a group of scholars, who put together a detailed study of the land, its monuments, and its history.

THE ROSETTA STONE

But the old records and inscriptions remained a mystery. The great breakthrough came by accident. Troops were building a new fort at Rosetta, near Alexandria, when a soldier dug up a broken slab of black rock. It was covered with writing in three different scripts—hieroglyphic, demotic (a simple kind of hieroglyphics), and Greek.

Jean-François Champollion, a brilliant scholar, compared the three kinds of writing. He could read Greek and managed to find the different forms of names such as "Ptolemy" and "Cleopatra" in each of the scripts. After years of work, Champollion built up a list of hieroglyphics and their meanings. At last, modern historians could read the records of the ancient Egyptians.

A RICH FIND
This photograph shows Howard Carter and Lo[rd] Carnarvon in 1922, standing at the entranc[e] to Tutankhamun's tomb[.] Their sensational discovery was the most important archaeologica[l] find of the century. The tomb was virtually untouched. Despite some evidence of robbers, the inner burial chamber had not been entered sin[ce] the pharaoh was placed there, over three thousan[d] years earlier.

THE BIRTH OF EGYPTOLOGY

The new discoveries led to a popular craze for Egyptian remains. Robbers worked even harder at ransacking tombs, and selling the precious objects inside to eager European collectors. But in the middle of the 19th century the Egyptian government at last realized what fabulous treasures it possessed. A Frenchman, Auguste Mariette, was put in charge of all excavations. He quickly stopped the wholesale pillaging of ancient sites and opened the first Egyptian museum, now housed in Cairo.

A new branch of study was born, called Egyptology. Enthusiasts, such as the American writer Amelia Edwards, helped to save what remained from ancient Egypt, and scholars such as Flinders Petrie developed new and more careful ways of excavating the sites. Petrie's aim was to uncover important information about this vast civilization, not just to look for treasure.

RAMESES' TOMB
The important work done by Champollion allowed later scholars to decipher the rich writings on the walls of tombs such as this one, which belonged to Rameses II.

AN AMAZING DISCOVERY

The most famous moment in Egyptology came in 1922. An archaeologist called Howard Carter had been painstakingly searching the Valley of the Kings in the hope of finding a tomb that had not been broken into. In November he came upon a step cut in the rock. It led down to a door bearing the seal of Tutankhamun, a king from the 18th Dynasty.

A few days later, Carter was able to break through to a second door and peer through a hole. "As my eyes grew accustomed to the light," he wrote, "details of the room within emerged slowly, strange animals, statues, and gold—everywhere the glint of gold." Inside was a staggering array of beautiful wooden and metal objects, from ebony beds and ivory thrones, to the three gold coffins that contained the pharaoh's mummified body.

This was not just the most valuable archaeological find ever made—although more than three thousand treasures were discovered. It was also one of the most important. The contents of the tomb had lain almost untouched since their burial. The objects gave modern historians an unrivaled glimpse into the royal world of the New Kingdom. Egyptologists are still examining and learning from the extraordinary hoard.

HISTORY IN STONE

There are many amazing discoveries from ancient Egypt. This civilization survived for three thousand years. During that vast time span, its daily life, language, religion, and art changed very little. The ancient Egyptians built massive temples and pyramids with only the simplest tools. They wrote the first books on medicine, they pioneered arithmetic, engineering, astronomy, and botany. They invented sundials and water clocks to tell the time. They even developed the first calendar with 365 days to a year (almost exactly like ours). But the most amazing fact of all is that so much of what they made has survived to this day.

STONE CALENDAR
This ancient Egyptian calendar shows how the Egyptians divided their year into 365 days.

REMAINS FROM THE PAST
Scientists examine a mummy from the Valley of the Kings.

LOOKING FOR CLUES

By studying all the remains, we can learn how the Egyptians lived and we can learn about great events that happened so long ago. Some of the most valuable evidence can be found in the smaller and broken remains—pieces of clay pots, ornaments, traces of food, and fragments of tools. For example, archaeologists can work out the age of a building or tomb by the type of pottery that is buried inside it.

An even more important source of knowledge are the written records on papyrus scrolls. Using hieroglyphics or (later) demotic writings, scribes recorded major dates and events, as well as the details of rituals such as the burial ceremony. Thanks to the discovery of the Rosetta Stone, we can now decipher what these ancient writings say.

OBELISK AT LUXOR
Hieroglyphics on pillars like this one have been decoded by scholars of Egyptology.

THE MAJOR SITES

The most exciting and impressive evidence of ancient Egypt is, of course, to be seen in the great monuments. This history in stone is still visited and explored by tourists and scholars every day. The Pyramids at Giza and the Temple at Karnak are some of the most breathtaking structures ever built. The whole stretch of Egypt, from the Delta south to the old site of the Cataract at Aswan, contains so many ruins that it would take a lifetime to explore them all.

ASWAN DAM

One vital part of ancient Egyptian life will never be seen again—the annual flood. In 1960 work began on a massive dam across the Nile at Aswan. It created a huge lake, which provides hydroelectricity for the villages. This huge dam has stopped the river from flooding. Farmers now use artificial fertilizer on their land instead of the natural silt. Several fine temples were moved so that they would not be sunk beneath the new lake.

KARNAK
Ancient Egyptian architecture at Karnak in Thebes.

THE SEARCH FOR KNOWLEDGE

Even if you do not travel to Egypt, there are many ways of seeing or finding out about its ancient history. The plundering of Egypt during the 19th century filled many museums throughout the world with Egyptian antiquities. Among others, there are wonderful things to see in the British Museum in London, the Louvre in Paris, the Agyptisches Museum in Berlin, and the Metropolitan Museum in New York. There are also many wonderful books about ancient Egypt and its treasures, as well as several websites on the subject.

Engineers, architects, historians, and scholars are still puzzling over the incredible monuments erected in ancient Egypt. The search for information and answers goes on. The discovery of history in stone continues to fascinate scholars and ordinary people alike as much today as in 1798, when ancient Egypt was, at last, after so many centuries, uncovered again.

TIME LINE OF ANCIENT EGYPT

circa 5000 B.C.
The first settlers arrive in the Nile Valley. They probably drove their animals from one watering hole to another.

circa 3200 B.C.
Menes (or Narmer) is the first pharaoh, after uniting Upper and Lower Egypt. He founds the city of Memphis.

circa 2686–2180 B.C.
This period, from the 4th Dynasty to the end of the 6th, is known now as the Old Kingdom. It was the age of the pyramids.

2600 B.C.
King Khufu orders the construction of the Great Pyramid at Giza—the biggest ever built.

2180 B.C.
The royal dynasty is weakened, while nobles and officials become more powerful. Civil war breaks out.

4000s B.C. Farming villages are founded in the Nile Valley.

2690 B.C. A step pyramid is built at Saqqara for king Djoser.

2680–2565 B.C. The main pyramids at Giza are built for kings Khufu, Khefre, and Menkaure. The small ones are for Menkaure's wives.

1570 B.C.
Ahmosis finally drives the Hyksos rulers out of Egypt and founds the 18th Dynasty.

circa 1570–1070 B.C.
This period, from the 18th Dynasty to the end of the 20th, is known as the New Kingdom.

1479 B.C.
Queen Hatshepsut, wife of Tuthmosis II, pushes aside her husband's son to become the first female pharaoh.

1367–1360 B.C.
Reign of Amenhotep IV. He changes his name to Akhenaten to honor the sun god, Aten. He bans the worship of many gods.

circa 1360 B.C.
Tutankhaten becomes king, aged nine, and changes his name to Tutankhamun.

circa 1478 B.C. The mortuary temple of Hatshepsut, a ruler of the 18th Dynasty, is built at Luxor.

1360s B.C. Akhenaten's chief wife is Nefertiti, whose name means "the beautiful one is come."

525 B.C.
Persians win the Battle of Pelusium and conquer Egypt. The Persians rule for nearly 200 years.

332 B.C.
Alexander the Great's army defeats the Persians. Alexander settles at Memphis, then founds Alexandria.

323 B.C.
Alexander the Great dies. The Macedonian commander Ptolemy becomes king and the Ptolemy Dynasty begins.

circa 280 B.C.
The great lighthouse at Alexandria is completed. The Pharos becomes one of the Seven Wonders of the World.

51 B.C.
Cleopatra seizes power from her brother, Ptolemy XIII, becoming the second female ruler of Egypt.

circa 290 B.C. Work begins on the Pharos lighthouse. It used fire to alert sailors at night.

circa 2061–1633 B.C.
This period, from the 7th Dynasty to the end of the 13th, is known as the Middle Kingdom. Thebes becomes Egypt's capital.

1990 B.C.
Building work begins on the Great Temple of Amun at Karnak.

1860 B.C.
12th-Dynasty kings (including Sesostris III) build lines of forts against attackers from the Delta and the south.

1782 B.C.
There is renewed civil war after the start of the weak 13th Dynasty. The Asiatic Hyksos take power in Egypt.

1600 B.C.
Strong Theban rulers begin their fight to expel the Hyksos.

The temple complex at Karnak is built during the Middle Kingdom, and renovated during the New Kingdom.

The center of worship for the sun god, Re, was the town of Heliopolis.

1275 B.C.
Rameses II halts the Hittite invasion at the Battle of Kadesh and wins back Syria.

1158 B.C.
Death of Rameses III, last of the great Egyptian kings.

1070 B.C.
There is chaos in Egypt, following a succession of weak kings. This leads to renewed civil war and Egypt is divided once again.

circa 1070–31 B.C.
During this time, various foreign powers take control of and rule Egypt.

663 B.C.
The Assyrians invade Egypt and sack the city of Thebes.

Rameses II ruled from 1304 B.C. until 1237 B.C.

1200s B.C. The temple at Abu Simbel is built to honor Rameses II.

31 B.C.
Cleopatra and Mark Antony are defeated by the Romans at Actium. Egypt becomes part of the Roman Empire.

A.D. 383
The Roman emperor Theodosius has all non-Christian temples in Egypt destroyed.

A.D. 639
Muslim armies invade Egypt. It becomes part of the Islamic Empire.

1798
French soldiers discover the Rosetta Stone. The scholar Champollion deciphers its hieroglyphics.

1922
Howard Carter discovers the tomb of Tutankhamun.

This mummy case from the first century A.D. mixes Egyptian tradition with realistic, Roman-style painting.

The vulture and cobra emblems on King Tutankhamun's death mask symbolize kingship.

GLOSSARY

A

agate A hard kind of precious stone.

amulet Something worn as a charm to ward off evil.

B

barren Unfit to grow plants or produce crops.

basalt A hard rock formed from the lava of volcanoes.

bronze An alloy (mixture) of copper and tin that is much harder than pure copper.

C

canopic jar Special ritual jar used to hold organs (heart, liver, etc.) of a mummified body.

Canopic jars.

cataract A very large waterfall with a long drop.

colonnade A row of columns.

composite bow A weapon made of two or more materials (wood, horn, etc.) glued together to make it stronger.

cult A system of religious worship, usually centering on one god or goddess.

D

delta The triangular-shaped deposit of silt and other materials that sometimes builds up at the mouth of a river.

dynasty A line or family of rulers who inherit power from each other.

Nile delta.

F

falcon A kind of hawk with long, pointed wings. Falcons are able to fly very fast.

flax A plant grown for the fibers in its stalks, which can be processed into linen cloth.

G

gazelle A small type of antelope.

Statue of the falcon god, Horus.

H

heir The person who inherits the property or title of someone else after their death. For instance, the pharaoh's eldest son was the heir to the throne of Egypt after the pharaoh died.

I

ibex A kind of wild goat.

image Portrait or statue of a person or god, used for worship and other rituals.

irrigation Diverting water from rivers or lakes into channels, to nourish planted crops in dry areas.

ivory The hard, white material which makes up the tusks of elephants, hippopotamuses, and some other mammals.

L

loom A machine used for making cloth, by weaving two sets of threads at right angles.

M

mastaba A low and modest tomb used for the burial of lesser officials in ancient Egypt.

N

natron A mineral form of soda found in the desert and used to preserve mummified bodies.

nilometer
A stone gauge carved on the bank of the Nile River to show the depth of the water.

Nilometer.

nomarch Local official appointed by the pharaoh to rule a district or province.

O

obelisk A tapering stone pillar, usually rectangular and with a pyramidal point on top.

onyx A kind of hard quartz stone, with different layers of color.

Narmer palette.

P

palette A flat carving or molding, usually showing a figure or symbol.

papyrus A paper-like material made by pounding together the fibers of the papyrus reed.

plumb line A string with a weight on the end, which will hang down vertically and can be used to check the angle of walls.

pomegranate An edible fruit with a tough skin. Pomegranates contain a juicy red pulp and lots of seeds.

pulley A system of moving weights using a rope running through a wheel with a grooved rim.

pyramid A stone structure with a square base and sloping sides meeting at a point, or apex.

Stonemasons.

R

ritual A religious ceremony or service.

S

scarab A species of beetle, sacred to the ancient Egyptians.

Scarab.

silo A large pit or vessel for storing corn and other crops.

square A building tool with a set right angle. Squares are used to check whether corners are exactly square.

stonemason A craftsman who is skilled in shaping and building with stone.

V

vizier The country's second most powerful official after the king.

W

waterhole A water source (usually most valuable in desert areas) that rarely dries up.

The Great Pyramid.

INDEX

PHOTO CREDITS

Key: a = above, b = below, c = center, l = left, r = right.

British Museum 42/43ac, 43r; **Corel** 54bl; **Edimedia** 12ar, 18bl, 18/19bc, 21bl, 22l, 23bl & bc & cr, 25al & r, 26l, 27t & cr, 29br, 30b, 30/31ac, 34l, 37r, 39al, 42bl, 44bl, 45ac & br, 46l, 49al, 50/51ac, 52bl, 52/53ac, 55; **Edimedia/British Museum** 14bl, 24l, 32bl, 33cr, 38tr; **Edimedia/Victoria and Albert Museum** 16/17bc, 41br; **Edimedia/Jacques Marthelot** 8l, 11br, 12b, 14ar, 17ar, 20l, 28b, 40l, 44/45ac; **Gamma** 54br; **Image Select** 10bl, 24br, 25bc, 35ar, 39br, 47bl, 48l, 53br, 55br; **Image Select/Ann Ronan** 9br, 10/11ac, 13br, 16al, 17bc, 21ar, 23ac, 26/27bc, 34br, 36l, 41al, 44br, 47ar, 49br, 54al; **Spectrum Colour Library/D. & J. Heaton** 20/21ac.